Let's Start!
Science

Touch that!

Sally Hewitt

QED Publishing

QED

First published in the UK in 2005 by
QED Publishing
A Quarto Group company
226 City Road
London EC1V 2TT

www.qed-publishing.co.uk

A Catalogue record for this book is available
from the British Library.

ISBN 1 84538 447 4

Written by Sally Hewitt
Series Consultant Sally Morgan

Project Editor: Honor Head
Series Designer: Zeta Jones
Photographer: Michael Wicks
Picture Researcher: Nic Dean

Publisher: Steve Evans
Creative Director: Louise Morley
Editorial Manager: Jean Coppendale

Printed and bound in China

Picture credits:

CORBIS/Layne Kennedy 14, /Tom Stewart
15, /Peter Steiner 21;
FLPA/Minden Pictures 21;
Getty Images/Julie Toy/Taxi 6, /Gabrielle
Revere/Stone 8 /Will & Deni McIntyre/
Stone 10 /Timothy Shonnard/Stone 12/Wides
& Holl/Taxi 12.

The words in bold
like this are
explained in the
Glossary on page 22.

Contents

Feel this!

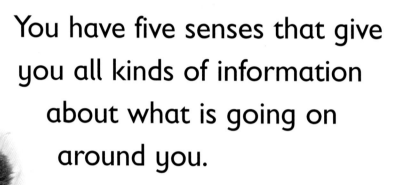

You have five senses that give you all kinds of information about what is going on around you.

The five senses are sight, touch, taste, smell and hearing. This book is about your sense of touch.

Touch helps you to feel if things are hard or soft, hot or cold …and what hurts!

What can you feel now? Do your clothes feel **ticklish** or scratchy?

Hmmm, feels very soft...

Are you holding something? What shape is it? Is it hard or squashy? Is it hot or cold?

▶ Your skin is the part of your body you feel with.

5

That's cold!

Your body is covered in skin from head to toe. Tiny **sensors** in your skin send messages from your skin to your brain.

Oooh, this floor is hard and cold!

Your brain tells you what you are feeling.

6

Your brain remembers what things feel like. It sends a message to tell you how the thing you are about to touch feels.

Activity

Can you remember what things feel like? Use these words to describe what the objects below feel like.

sharp   hot   rough   smooth   soft
         cold   hard

Which are dangerous to touch?

Feels nice

The skin on some parts of your body is more **sensitive** than others. That means it has more feeling.

▲ Babies feel new things with their fingers and mouth!

Your lips, tongue, fingers and toes are very sensitive.

◀ The tips of your fingers have lots of sensors.

Some parts of your skin have only a few sensors so they are not very sensitive.

How sensitive is your skin? Ask a friend to shut their eyes. With a hairbrush, lightly touch their knee, elbow, back, cheek and hand. Ask them to squeak as soon as they feel something.

Which parts of their skin are not very sensitive?

Hands and feet

Your fingers need to be able to feel so that you can do things such as write, hold a pencil and tie your shoe laces.

▲ Blind people read by feeling raised dots with their fingertips.

Could you play a game like this without any feeling in your fingertips?

Your feet are very sensitive, too. They can be very ticklish.

Test how sensitive your feet are. Ask a friend to put some objects on the floor. Shut your eyes and feel them with your bare feet.

Can you tell what they are? How well can you feel with your feet?

11

Touch

Your skin can feel very light touches like the brush of a feather and the drizzle of rain.

What other very light touches can you feel?

◀ Tickling is a light touch that makes you giggle!

You feel a hard touch or squeeze deep inside your skin. A very hard touch gives you a bruise!

If something squeezes your skin for a long time, such as sock elastic, you stop noticing it.

Shut your eyes. Can you point to where the top of your socks are pressing against your legs?

Ouch!

When you feel **pain**, you just want it to go away!

But pain is very important because it helps to keep you safe.

Pain teaches you not to touch things that burn, prickle, cut and sting!

▸ A bandage protects your skin while it heals.

Ouch, that hurts!

As soon as you touch something that hurts, a message is sent to your brain warning 'danger'!

You move away before you are badly hurt.

▶ You remember things that have hurt you and keep away from them.

Shape and size

Look around you. You can probably name most of the things you see. Can you tell what things are when you can't see them but you can only feel them?

Ask a friend to put some objects in a bag. Choose things like a teaspoon, pencil, rubber and coin.

◀ A coin feels round, hard and flat. A rubber feels smooth and squashy.

Feeling the shape of something helps you to know what it is. Its size helps you, too.

Find a marble, a ping-pong ball, a golf ball and a tennis ball. They are all the same shape but different sizes. Shut your eyes.

Can you tell what they are by feeling them? Put them in order of size.

Rough and smooth

Your skin can feel if things are rough or smooth. A pineapple is covered in spiky bumps. It feels rough.

An apple feels smooth.

Rough and smooth are different **textures**.

◀ This picture has many textures. There is smooth paper and rough cardboard. What else can you see?

The mirror feels smooth.

Activity

Guess if things in your house feel rough or smooth just by looking at them.

Feel them and see if you were right. What about a cushion, a spoon and a sponge?

This brush feels rough.

Feelers

Where is everybody?

In the dark, you can't see so you feel the way. You put your hands out so you don't bump into things.

You test the ground with your foot for steps or holes so you don't trip over.

Animals have different ways of feeling the world around them.

A cat feels with its sensitive whiskers.

A snail reaches out with its **feelers**, to feel the way.

An elephant feels with the tip of its trunk.

Glossary

Feelers

Some animals have feelers such as antennae or tentacles to feel what is going on around them.

Pain

You feel pain if something hurts when it touches you. Hot, cold and sharp things can feel painful.

Sensitive

Your skin is sensitive to the things you touch. Some parts of your skin are more sensitive than others.

Sensors

Sensors in your skin send messages to your brain about what you are feeling.

Texture

Texture is what the outside, or skin, of something feels like. The texture of an apple is smooth, the texture of a pineapple is rough.

Ticklish

Parts of your skin are very sensitive and ticklish. It makes you giggle when they are touched lightly or tickled.

Index

Parents' and teachers' notes

- Find words throughout the book about texture such as soft, scratchy, rough and smooth. Make a collection of objects, scraps of paper and material. Ask the children to describe them and then sort them by texture.

- Write these pairs of words on four cards: soft and rough, hard and smooth, soft and smooth, hard and rough. Now find a sponge, an apple, a silky scarf and a pumice stone. Ask the children to feel the objects, then find the pair of words that describes them.

- Make a collage using materials with different textures. Make pictures using scraps of material such as velvet, denim, wool, card and sandpaper.

- Make a witch's brew. In the dark, give out things such as cold, cooked spaghetti, a damp tea bag, a peeled grape and a shrivelled carrot. Ask the children to feel them and imagine what spooky things the witch might be putting in her brew. Turn on the light and see what she has cooked up!

- Look at pictures of animals, including insects. Do they have furry or scaly skin? How do they feel the world around them? Which animals have whiskers, antennae or tentacles?

- Talk about touching things safely. Discuss some questions children should ask themselves before they touch anything, such as is it sharp, hot or cold? Is there moving machinery that could trap their hands? Talk about not touching paintings in a gallery or plants in a garden.

- Make a touch chart. Collect drawings and photographs of things that are nice, horrid or dangerous to touch. Sort and stick them onto three large sheets of paper. Make a collection of words to add to the pictures that describe what they feel like.